SEASIDE

The Francis Frith Collection

First published in the United Kingdom in 2006 by
The Francis Frith Collection®

ISBN 1-84589-086-8

British Library Cataloguing in Publication Data

Francis Frith's 50 Classics - Seaside.
Compiled by Terence and Eliza Sackett

The Francis Frith Collection
Frith's Barn, Teffont,
Salisbury, Wiltshire SP3 5QP
Tel: +44 (0) 1722 716 376
Email: info@francisfrith.co.uk
www.francisfrith.co.uk

Printed and bound in India

Front Cover: **TENBY**, South Sands 1890 28050t *The colour-tinting is for illustrative purposes only, and is not intended to be historically accurate*

FRANCIS FRITH
VICTORIAN PIONEER

Francis Frith, founder of the world-famous photographic archive, was a complex and multi-talented man. A devout Quaker and a highly successful Victorian businessman, he was philosophic by nature and pioneering in outlook. By 1855 he had already established a wholesale grocery business in Liverpool, and sold it for the astonishing sum of £200,000, which is the equivalent today of over £15,000,000. Now in his thirties, and captivated by the new science of photography, Frith set out on a series of pioneering journeys up the Nile and to the Near East.

INTRIGUE AND EXPLORATION

He was the first photographer to venture beyond the sixth cataract of the Nile. Africa was still the mysterious 'Dark Continent', and Stanley and Livingstone's historic meeting was a decade into the future. The conditions for picture taking confound belief. He laboured for hours in his wicker dark-room in the sweltering heat of the desert, while the volatile chemicals fizzed dangerously in their trays. Back in London he exhibited his photographs and was 'rapturously cheered' by members of the Royal Society. His reputation as a photographer was made overnight.

VENTURE OF A LIFE-TIME

By the 1870s the railways had threaded their way across the country, and Bank Holidays and half-day Saturdays had been made obligatory by Act of Parliament. All of a sudden the working man and his family were able to enjoy days out, take holidays, and see a little more of the world.

With typical business acumen, Francis Frith foresaw that these new tourists would enjoy having souvenirs to commemorate their days out. For the next thirty years he travelled the country by train and by pony and trap, producing fine photographs of seaside resorts and beauty spots that were keenly bought by millions of Victorians.

These prints were painstakingly pasted into family albums and pored over during the dark nights of winter, rekindling precious memories of summer excursions. Frith's studio was soon supplying retail shops all over the country, and by 1890 F Frith & Co had become the greatest specialist photographic publishing company in the world, with over 2,000 sales outlets, and pioneered the picture postcard.

FRANCIS FRITH'S LEGACY

Francis Frith had died in 1898 at his villa in Cannes, his great project still growing. The archive he created continued in business for another seventy years. By 1970 it contained over a third of a million pictures showing 7,000 British towns and villages.

Frith's legacy to us today is of immense significance and value, for the magnificent archive of evocative photographs he created provides a unique record of change in the cities, towns and villages throughout Britain over a century and more.

Frith and his fellow studio photographers revisited locations many times down the years to update their views, compiling for us an enthralling and colourful pageant of British life and character.

We are fortunate that Frith was dedicated to recording the minutiae of everyday life. For it is this sheer wealth of visual data, the painstaking chronicle of changes in dress, transport, street layouts, buildings, housing, engineering and landscape that captivates us so much today, offering us a powerful link with the past and with the lives of our ancestors.

Computers have now made it possible for Frith's many thousands of images to be accessed almost instantly. The archive offers every one of us an opportunity to examine the places where we and our families have lived and worked down the years. Its images, depicting our shared past, are now bringing pleasure and enlightenment to millions around the world a century and more after his death.

INTRODUCTION

The text accompanying these photographs is extracted from a late Victorian tourist guidebook to the seaside resorts of Britain. It offers a true picture of the preoccupations and attitudes of its period. Resorts and individual features are therefore referred to in the present tense, and the original spelling and punctuation have been retained for the purposes of authenticity.

'We love our haunts by the sea; the poorest among us regards his favourite resort pretty much as the rich man does his country seat ... How the eyes brighten at the sight of a familiar spot! And how vividly the old associations crowd back to the mind – memories of glowing careless days, that gave new life to the jaded worker, and caused the brain-weary to forget their ineffable tedium vitae'.

The words and pictures in this book inevitably recall an age that is long since gone. Yet they bring us a strong reminder of the simple and diverse pleasures that the old-style British resort offered to many generations of tourists.

Redcar dates from 1842, since when it has progressed at quite an extraordinary rate, and it certainly owes much to its magnificent sweep of sands. They are ten miles in length and a mile broad at low water, and they have been characterised as 'smooth as velvet, yet so firm that neither horse not man leave their imprint on them as they tread the strand'.

This has been called 'the Queen of English watering-places'. The Victorians loved all sorts of entertainment, especially music. Travelling showmen were a common sight. Here the minstrels seem to be collecting money from the crowd standing on the beach waiting for the show to begin.

SCARBOROUGH, THE BAY 1886 18240

2

This prosperous watering-place was once an insignificant fishing village. Its picturesque position on the cliffs of one of the noblest bays on the east coast of England, and its fine beach, along with its splendid hotels and handsome private houses, make Filey one of the most attractive resorts in the United Kingdom.

3

FILEY, THE PROMENADE 1901 48018

Bridlington Quay is one of the less pretentious neighbours of Scarborough, sharing its advantages of situation and climate, but without its rather expensive gaieties. The sands are all that family parties can desire. Bridlington is protected by Flamborough Head, the lion of the neighbourhood, whose airy heights are accessible by an hour's walk or by regular conveyances.

Skegness sprung up into considerable note since the extension of the railway in 1873. The great attraction is the firm wide sands, on which donkeys, swings, cocoanut-shies, and other amusements for excursionists will be found in full activity during the season. From the sand hills along the shore there are extensive views over the German Ocean. Fine sunsets may be watched hence.

On the north-west angle of the coast of Norfolk stands the pretty watering-place of Hunstanton St Edmunds, which, during the summer months, is crowded with visitors, the rooms, which out of the season can be got for five shillings, fetching a guinea a week, or more. The little town is perched upon a hill: the western side forms a picturesque sea-cliff.

HUNSTANTON, THE GREEN 1907 58895

6

Cromer stands high and bracing on its breezy cliffs, from which stairs and zig-zag paths lead down to the sands. On undeveloped tastes Cromer would be thrown away. The cliffs are brown and sandy, the sea blue and the landscape of a universal green. You can wander for miles along the cliffs amongst such a variety of wild flowers as is rarely seen collected together.

CROMER, THE SANDS 1906 56855

Yarmouth's attractions include firm and extensive sands for bathers, a marine parade, three piers, the Theatre Royal, and an aquarium. Although it styles itself Great Yarmouth to distinguish it from that small Yarmouth in the Isle of Wight, its usual associations are less with greatness than with bigness, boisterousness, and a joviality unrestrained by any false pride.

Felixstowe has of late years risen rapidly. The visit of the German Imperial Family certainly did much for the place by proclaiming the merits of its sea-bathing: but what has chiefly helped to bring this resort into prominence is the adjacent golf links, now renowned as among the best in England.

Southend is reached in little more than an hour by the excellent trains of the Great Eastern Railway. It is quite remarkable to see the crowds of Londoners poured into Southend by steamboat and excursion train on a fine summer's day. The pier is a mile and a quarter in length; one may be conveyed right out to sea by the electric tramway, which runs down the pier in five minutes.

SOUTHEND, THE BEACH 1898 41383

10

There is no affectation, no blasé cynicism about your genuine Margate visitors. Its sands are thronged by a crowd of idlers ready to be easily entertained by jugglers, Punch and Judy shows, and wandering minstrels. There are busy vendors of refreshments and knick-knacks; family parties, encamped with umbrellas and novels; eager children, sprawling babies and their nurses, and scores of adventurous youngsters seriously labouring in the sand with spade and wheelbarrow.

MARGATE, THE SANDS 1906 54758

Modest little Broadstairs needs no defending, having powerful patrons, the most illustrious of whom was Charles Dickens, whose residence at 'Bleak House' is still pointed out as the chief monument of the place the great novelist liked so well. Broadstairs still remains quieter and more select than its larger and noisier neighbours, and is especially in high favour with family parties, who find quite a little paradise on the sheltered beach.

From the end of the pier Ramsgate looks very well indeed. At night, when the winding, sloping streets light their lamps, and the hotels and cafes around the harbour are alive with visitors, one might almost fancy that one was in a lively foreign seaport, especially as all the world is abroad to take the cool evening air, and the French boatmen are heard chattering in their own tongue.

Dover is about two hours from London by express train. During the summer months there is a good service of steamboats between this interesting watering-place and London. Shakespeare's Cliff commands a broad view of the shores of France. It is about 350 feet above the level of the sea; its height is supposed to have been greatly diminished by bits of rock falling from its summit.

The increase of the houses of visitors must tend to spoil the original individuality of a population, but in Hastings these qualities are preserved to an unusual extent, especially among the fishermen. Under the East Cliff, 'Dutch' fish auctions are often held. The steep, turfy slopes of its East and West Hills have recently been made more accessible by means of a lift. The bathing here is excellent in every way.

HASTINGS, THE BEACH 1925 77979

To convey any notion at all of this watering-place to those who have never visited it, one must mention that there are noble tree-planted streets and shady avenues, an imposing sea-front of about three miles, an excellent beach of mingled sand and shingle, a pier of the most approved pattern, an abundance of seats and shelters, gardens and promenades, and irreproachable sanitary arrangements and water supply.

This famous watering-place owes its present prosperity to Dr Russell, of Lewes, who removed hence in 1750. He published a treatise on the advantages of sea-bathing, recommending Brighton very strongly. You can scarcely move on the Parade on a fine afternoon without meeting troops of fair horse-women attended by their riding-masters. The stream of carriages is almost as incessant as on a Drawing Room day at Buckingham Palace.

That Worthing has a milder climate than its neighbours is shown by the large quantities of fruit and vegetables which it sends to Covent Garden. The sands are smooth and hard, and their condition during the summer months has been graphically described as one long mile of nursery. There are many people who prefer this watering-place to Brighton, on the grounds that it is quieter and far more economical to live in.

WORTHING, CHILDREN ON THE SANDS 1906 56709 **18**

About 1785, Sir Richard Hotham, a wealthy Southwark hatter, who determined upon acquiring the glory of a seaside Romulus, set to work to erect a town of first-class villas in this pleasant spot, with a view to creating a truly recherché watering-place, to be known to posterity as Hothampton. He spent £60,000; he erected and furnished some really commodious villas, but did not succeed in giving his name to his own creation.

Littlehampton lies between Worthing and Bognor; and it is, perhaps, quieter than either; children will find a paradise upon its sands, with nothing from which they can contrive to tumble; and some older young folk may be inclined to grumble if asked to spend their holiday there — though there can be no doubt that Littlehampton has grown far livelier within the last few years.

LITTLEHAMPTON, THE PROMENADE 1903 50215

20

As practically the west-end of Portsmouth, Southsea holds a unique position among watering-places. It would not be rustic or romantic enough for all tastes, but recommends itself to many by the stir of military and naval life. What with regimental bands, parades, and reviews by land, and the Solent continually alive with yachts, steamboats, and battleships, it can never be dull.

This is the capital of the Underclift. Its popularity is due to the remarkable salubrity of its climate, and the singular beauty of its situation. Forty years ago, its few inhabitants were nearly all fishermen. Now we have hotels, churches, shops, cottages and villas in every conceivable style and every outrageous shape. From the Esplanade there extends a fine pier, erected in 1887, from which steamboat excursions may be made.

VENTNOR, THE ESPLANADE 1908 60527

22

LINNINGTON'S
HYGIENIC
BATHING TENTS
FOR
MIXED BATHING

Since the opening of the railway, Swanage has vastly increased in favour as a watering-place; it is situated in a beautiful bay, and commands a glorious prospect of down and sea and cliff. The town of Swanage is unpretending, and its patrons will be those who do not crave for gaiety. The great interest in the neighbourhood is for the geologist: upwards of sixty quarries of Purbeck stone have contributed to St Paul's Cathedral.

From the ever-green valley of the Bourne (whence arose the nucleus of this resort) Bournemouth stretches for miles in either direction upon the sandy cliffs and pine-clad table-land of a gently curving bay, broken by picturesque chines. Nothing can be more snug and luxuriant than the mouth of the valley, which is here being turned into a long strip of garden, blooming with arbutus, rhododendrons and other choice shrubs.

BOURNEMOUTH, FROM THE PIER 1897 40559

This popular watering-place is very pleasantly situated. The coast here, turning to the south, forms a wide, open bay. The esplanade extends for about a mile, and is lined with elegant houses and defended by a substantial sea-wall. At the northern end are the Green Hill Gardens, and at the southern end, the Alexandra Gardens; while near the clock tower stands an equestrian statue of George III, erected in 1809.

This charmingly-situated little watering-place lies in a sheltered valley, and its garden-girt villas are further beautified by a sparkling brook, spanned by numerous rustic bridges. Myrtles and hydrangeas bloom lustily in the open air in this delightful spot. The beach is famous for its prettily-marked pebbles. Thanks to the absence of the railway, this charming little spot retains much of its primitive simplicity.

A celebrated art critic has declared that Edinburgh, Venice and Torquay are the three most beautiful towns in Europe. This celebrated and fashionable winter resort occupies the northern corner of Tor Bay, and is securely sheltered from all winds, except those from the south-east. Torquay is a town of charming villas, which, amphitheatre-like, stretch upwards from the shore in terraces to the higher ground overlooking the sea.

TORQUAY, THE BOWLING GREEN 1906 54024

27

Of late Paignton has been greatly improved; a promenade pier has been erected, and the Esplanade – on which there is a band-stand – greatly extended. This charming resort should be visited in the apple blossoming season, for the cider apple is largely cultivated in the neighbourhood, and cider is manufactured on a large scale. Paignton possesses splendid climate and remarkably fine sands. The bathing, too, is excellent.

The old town, quaint and picturesque, is situated on the low ground near the edge of the harbour, and as a matter of course, the streets are very narrow. The new portion of the town lies for the most part on high ground, and the commodious houses and charming terraces overlook the magnificent harbour on the one side and the English Channel on the other.

FALMOUTH, THE MARKET STRAND 1890 24208

Penzance is celebrated as a watering-place on account of its mild climate, which makes it the resort of invalids suffering from pulmonary complaints. The old town, spread picturesquely round part of Mount's Bay, has delightfully narrow streets that ascend the hill from the fine esplanade at the edge of the sea. Penzance is frequently enlivened by the departure of the fleet of the fishing-boats for which the district is famed.

PENZANCE, ON THE ROCKS 1906 56513

The Great Western Railway found Newquay a small and almost inaccessible Cornish fishing village, and have transformed it into quite a fashionable seaside resort. The splendid sandy beach, which is so firm that tennis may be played on it, extends eastward for three miles beneath a range of beautiful cliffs. The long, crested waves dash themselves against the keen-edged rocks, and the misty rain and salt spray drive inland before the wind.

The bathing arrangements here are peculiar. At Crewkhorne one passes under the Runnycleaves by a dark tunnel that casts a shade of serious resolve upon the would-be bather, and on the hottest day inspires a shiver premonitory of the coming plunge. This cavernous-like entrance opens out into a picturesque cove, containing two walled-in bathing pools for ladies and gentlemen.

In addition to pure air, Weston has an unlimited supply of pure water from a never-failing spring, owned by the town, which is said to have its source in the Mendip range of hills. There are lovely roads and drives in the immediate neighbourhood, notably through the woods, and around Worlebury Hill. The town possesses one of the most extensive, and certainly one of the safest, bathing beaches in the kingdom.

Clevedon's immunity from the heavy excursion element which affects many seaside towns renders it a veritable haven of rest. The most popular and fashionable part of the promenade is that known as the Green Beach. It consists of an extensive plateau of greensward, about 40ft above the shelving beach, and provided with an elegant band-stand, a plantation, and a very handsome drinking-fountain.

Penarth was, until quite recently, merely the marine residence and bathing resort of the well-to-do inhabitants of Cardiff; now, however, it bids fair to become of far more than local importance. Of late, considerable improvements have been made. Frequent steamboats ply across the harbour when the tide serves. On the breezy cliff, fine pleasure grounds have been laid out. The Windsor Gardens, above the esplanade, afford pleasant walks and views.

PENARTH, THE PIER 1896 38461

35

Tenby stands on a tongue of limestone rock, ending a green promontory, which is crowned by the ruins of the old castle, and is now pleasantly laid out with walks which serve at once as pier and promenade, and from which are commanded fine views of the bays on either hand, and of the distant Devonshire coast opposite. Both on the north and south sands there are numerous bathing machines.

This is pre-eminently one of those places which have to be 'discovered', so to speak, by the roving holiday-maker. A tourist not infrequently takes considerable trouble to find out some charming seaside village in which he may dream out his few brief weeks of leisure in ineffable content and rest, soothed by the ever-present, placid sea, the rugged, flower-clad cliffs, and the charming, old-world life that goes on around him.

LYDSTEP, THE BEACH 1890 28010

Since the completion of the railway, great improvements have been made here, one of the most important being the construction of Victoria Terrace, by which means the Marine Terrace has been completed. The pride of Aberystwyth is its ruined castle, crumbling upon a rocky promontory against whose sides the waves of every tide are dashed with a force that threatens eventually to sweep away the whole.

The sands, which are extensive enough to give the full benefit of ozone to those who avail themselves of its health-giving properties, form an excellent bathing-ground, entirely free from danger. Hence Rhyl has become noted for the number of children that visit it, and these little ones find an inexhaustible fund of pleasure on its beach. The iron pier was built in 1867.

RHYL, THE BEACH 1913 65731

39

Pwllheli possesses perhaps the finest sandy beach in Wales; and there can be no doubt it will become one of the most attractive seaside places in the kingdom. The air is delightful, and the sanitary arrangements all that could be desired. The South Beach Land and Building Corporation Limited are building very extensively; and hotels, boarding and private houses are now being erected very rapidly.

Llanfairfechan is regarded with increasing favour by tourists and holiday-makers, who frequent the out-of-the-way parts of Wales. This charming little watering-place may be described as having a wooded and well-sheltered situation at the foot of the Penmaenmawr Mountain, and with a singularly lovely seaward prospect.

LLANFAIRFECHAN, THE SANDS 1890 23212

41

Llandudno stands back against the mass of the Great Orme's head, which shelters it from north winds, and on a neck of sand between two bays, which are so close together that in rough weather their spray meets over the town. The outer bay has a fine sweep, fringed with a long promenade and crescent extending towards the lower and more broken heights of the Little Orme.

Of the fine climate of Colwyn Bay there can be no doubt whatsoever. Flowers bloom here until well on towards Christmas, and are out again in some profusion in February. The gently-sloping sands extend for a mile or two, and are perfectly safe for children; while the deep water wherein the expert swimmer loves to disport himself is not too far out to be tiresome.

COLWYN BAY, ON THE SANDS 1898 42375

43

This is the chief Mersey bathing-place, which at once gains and loses by its proximity to the great commercial city of Liverpool. There are here a commodious pier, and a sandy beach well supplied with bathing machines, donkeys, minstrels, and the like attractions for the amusement of the Bank Holiday crowds. The pier affords fine views of the shipping and docks of Liverpool, the Irish Sea, and the mountains of Wales.

NEW BRIGHTON, THE LIGHTHOUSE 1892 30413

Blackpool has two piers, and everything handsome about her. Both are large; the north one is the more select, and the south more popular – just a penny pier where dancing goes on all day in the summer. The promenade is lighted by electricity, and has an electric tramway. Not to be left behind in any respect, Blackpool now has an Eiffel Tower of its own.

MORECAMBE, THE CENTRAL PIER 1888 21080

Morecambe is much frequented by trippers from the busy towns of Lancashire and Yorkshire, for whose recreation are provided abundant entertainments of distinctly popular order. There are swimming-baths and assembly rooms — of a sort — a People's Palace, and a few other places of amusement, chiefly conducted on music-hall lines. There is a large pier, a tramway, and a kind of Rosherville Garden with a lake for boating.

At Douglas, passengers can land at all states of the tide. The bay has been compared by local enthusiasts to the Bay of Naples, because at night a long crescent of lights is seen rising from the water. On the south side are the handsome stone piers, and a deep harbour cutting off most of the town from the cliffs of Douglas Head. Here lies the old town, whose narrow and crooked streets have been cloaked by the fine sea front.

A scattering of mansions, cottages, and odds and ends of streets nestling beneath a limestone cliff or half hidden away among wooded slopes, this tiny Torquay of Lancashire has, as yet, escaped the notice it fairly deserves. Except at high tide, we find here an expanse of mud and wet channelled sand, where bathers and boaters are fain, indeed, to snatch a fleeting joy.

Rothesay is the chief town of the County of Bute, and is situated in a well-formed bay, which affords safe anchorage in high wind. A fine esplanade faces the bay, and is laid out with much taste; it commands many beautiful views of Loch Striven. In the centre of the town are the ruins of Rothesay Castle, once a royal residence, and said to have been built about the year 1100.

ROTHESAY, THE ESPLANADE 1897 39837

49

Largs is a fine clean town, with several large churches. There are a great number of excellent houses for summer visitors, besides handsome and comfortable residential villas in the neighbourhood. There is now a golf course here; and the shelter afforded by the Great Cumbrae makes Largs a first-rate place for boating. Largs commands a magnificent view of Arran.

50

LARGS, THE CHURCH OF ST COLUMBA 1897 39855

INDEX

FREE PRINT OF YOUR CHOICE

Choose any Frith photograph in this book.

Simply complete the Voucher opposite and return it with your remittance for £2.25 (to cover postage and handling) and we will print the photograph of your choice in SEPIA (size 11 x 8 inches) and supply it in a cream mount with a burgundy rule line (overall size 14 x 11 inches).

Please note: photographs with a reference number starting with a "Z" are not Frith photographs and cannot be supplied under this offer.

Offer valid for delivery to one UK address only.

PLUS: **Order additional Mounted Prints at HALF PRICE - £7.49 each** (normally £14.99)

If you would like to order more Frith prints from this book, possibly as gifts for friends and family, you can buy them at half price (with no additional postage and handling costs).

PLUS: **Have your Mounted Prints framed**

For an extra £14.95 per print you can have your mounted print(s) framed in an elegant polished wood and gilt moulding, overall size 16 x 13 inches (no additional postage and handling required).

FRITH PRODUCTS AND SERVICES

All Frith photographs are available for you to buy as framed or mounted prints. From time to time, other illustrated items such as Address Books and Maps are also available. Already, almost 100,000 Frith archive photographs can be viewed and purchased on the internet through the Frith website.

For more detailed information on Frith companies and products, visit:

www.francisfrith.co.uk

Mounted Print
Overall size 14 x 11 inches (355 x 280mm)

IMPORTANT!

These special prices are only available if you use this form to order. You must use the ORIGINAL VOUCHER (no copies permitted).

We can only despatch to one UK address. This offer cannot be combined with any other offer.

For further information, contact:

The Francis Frith Collection, Frith's Barn, Teffont, Salisbury SP3 5QP

Tel: +44 (0) 1722 716 376

Fax: +44 (0) 1722 716 881

Email: sales@francisfrith.co.uk

Send completed Voucher form to:

The Francis Frith Collection, Frith's Barn, Teffont, Salisbury, Wiltshire SP3 5QP England

If you need more space, please write your address on a separate sheet of paper.

Voucher

for FREE and Reduced Price Frith Prints

Do not photocopy this voucher. Only the original is valid, so please fill it in, cut it out and return it to us with your order.

Picture ref no	Page number	Qty	Mounted @ £7.49	Framed + £14.95	Order Total £
1		1	Free of charge*	£	£
2			£7.49	£	£
3			£7.49	£	£
4			£7.49	£	£
5			£7.49	£	£
6			£7.49	£	£

Please allow 28 days for delivery.
Offer available to one UK address only

	* Post & handling	£ 2.25
	Total Order Cost	£

Title of this book . . . .

I enclose a cheque / postal order for £ . . . .
payable to 'The Francis Frith Collection'

OR debit my Mastercard / Visa / Maestro card

Card Number

Issue No (Maestro only)   Valid from (Maestro)

Expires   Signature

Name Mr/Mrs/Ms . . . .

Address . . . .

. . . .

. . . . Postcode . . . .

Daytime Tel No . . . .

E-mail . . . .

ISBN 1-84589-086-8   Valid to 31/12/08